Blackwell Education

First published 1989
© Bill Ridgway 1989
Illustrations copyright © Basil Blackwell 1989

Illustrations by Stuart Bristow, Bicester Community College

Published by Basil Blackwell Ltd
108 Cowley Road
Oxford OX4 1JF
England

All rights reserved. No part of this publication may be reproduced, stored in a retrieval system, or transmitted, in any form or by any means, electronic, mechanical, photocopying, recording or otherwise, without the prior permission of the publisher.

ISBN 0 631 90372 0

Printed in Great Britain by
Dotesios Printers Ltd, Trowbridge, Wiltshire

All the fun of the fair

You won't know me. I work in the new fair at Blackpool. They call it a leisure complex, but to me it's just a fair with a few new rides. I've worked on the fairs for a long time now. It's like any other job. You have your good days and your bad days. You have to take the rough with the smooth no matter what you do. Isn't that right?

It isn't the most exciting job in the world. Just day-to-day repairs. I'm an electrician by trade. That's why they took me on. But I can turn my hand to most things.

From time to time things get a bit boring, like any job. Sometimes you're rushed off your feet. In August I don't know whether I'm coming or going. It's like a madhouse.

It was like that last week. But not because of the breakdowns. Something happened that put a bit of excitement back into the job. It happened right here, in the fair – sorry, in the leisure complex. There were these five kids who came down with their folks looking for a good time. I was involved myself in a small way. Lennie told me the rest. He was one of the five . . .

* * * * *

'I think we should get back to the van,' Lennie said. 'I'm feeling hungry.'

He stood up, pulling on his shirt. A cool breeze had sprung up. Sal shook the sand out of her towel while Lola packed the bag.

'You coming or what?' Lennie said to Elvis, who had been dreaming while the others were packing.

He looked up. 'You're off, then?'

'We're off then.'

They walked up to the prom. There was a sea of people. They stood by the wall.

'I fancy chish and fips,' said Tim, the one with the jokes. 'How about you?'

'Not a bad idea,' Lennie said. 'That OK?' No one seemed to care. 'Right. Fish and chips for five.'

They got carried along by the crowd and crossed the road by the Golden Cod. It was getting on for ten o'clock, and a lot of people had the same idea: fish and chips for supper. The queue stretched from the counter and out through the front door.

'Elvis's turn,' said Lennie.

'I went last time,' Elvis said.

'He'll get it all wrong,' said Lola. 'Come on, give us your money. Sal and I will queue up. OK Sal?'

Sal shrugged. 'I suppose so.'

Once they'd eaten, they spent some time watching the crowds go by. It was dark when Lennie said he knew a quick way back to the caravan site.

'Forget the front,' he said. 'We'll use the back streets. Miss the crush.'

Lennie spoke in that way of his, like he was in charge and what he said went. He didn't mean it that way. But that's how it came over. The rest followed – apart from Lola. She was a match for Lennie, and had a mind of her own.

'We'll get lost,' she said. 'You sure you know the way?'

'Sure I'm sure.'

'What's wrong with crowds anyway? I like a bit of life.'

'Haven't you seen enough of people? Tell you what, we'll throw a coin – and mine's heads.'

The coin spun. Heads it was. The back streets.

'So Lennie wins again,' jeered Lola. 'Big deal.'

The street lamps were dim. Behind them, above the roof tops, the lights on the front flared. A thousand coloured bulbs flickered on and off. But where they walked was quiet and still. The streets were empty, the windows dark.

'This place gives me the creeps,' said Lola. 'I should never have let you talk me into it. I hope you know what you're doing.'

'Into the pit of doom,' joked Tim. 'Remember it, Lennie?'

Earlier that year Lennie had got Tim out of an old pit shaft. He'd been the hero of Deckford.

'We turn right here,' Lennie said, ignoring him.
'This is the way.'
A dark pool of shadow hid the turning. Far away they could hear music. It was coming from the fair. They finished off their chips as they walked.
'I'm tired,' Sal moaned. 'How far is it?'
She could be moody, but Lennie knew how to handle her.
'Not far, Sal. We're nearly there. You all right back there, Elvis? . . . Elvis?'
They looked back. Elvis was standing some way back, looking up at a large building.
'Come on, Elvis. Stop dreaming,' Lennie shouted.

Elvis came up.
'Did you see that place?'
No one answered.
'They must be working late. There's a light on.'
'So there's a light on,' mocked Sally. 'So what?'
'It's like a garage. There's a big door. There's a van outside,' said Elvis, all in a rush.
'Fancy that! A door in a house. And a van. What next!'
'OK, Sal. No need to be like that,' said Lennie. 'I shouldn't worry too much,' he added, turning to Elvis. 'Maybe someone left the light on.'
'I'm not worried, Lennie,' Elvis said. 'I was just saying, that's all.'

They carried on down the street for a few minutes before

Lennie decided he'd made a mistake. They'd come the wrong way. He laughed at their moaning and turned back the way they'd come. This time it was Lola who got left behind. She had a pair of new shoes. They were rubbing her heel. The plaster she put on earlier must have come off.
'I'm just fixing my shoe,' she called. 'I'll catch you up.'

The others faded into the night. She wished she'd left her shoes till later. The street shone dimly in the lamp-light. When the fairground music stopped she could hear the faraway voices of the crowds by the sea.

She found a new plaster and put her shoe back on. The others were nowhere to be seen. Then, as she stood up, she suddenly heard a faint noise to her right. She had stopped by the building with the light on. The sound had come from there. However, it was not the noise that scared her but the man at her side. He was standing by an open door, not two feet away, a large candlestick in his hand. He had taken a step towards the van when he bumped into her. In a second she had taken in the man's face, his bald head, his small, dark eyes, his ugly mouth. And at that moment he let out a startled cry and dropped the candlestick. She found herself running away from him. She heard him shout once. But she was already turning the corner at the far end of the street.

* * * * *

'Hey, steady,' Lennie shouted.
They had turned as they heard her running up behind them. 'Don't worry,' he laughed. 'We won't leave you behind.' She was not smiling. 'Something wrong?' he asked.
Lola tried to get her breath back. She pointed the way she had come. They turned and saw the man in the dim light. He was standing on the corner of the street. While they looked, he turned and walked away.
'Was he following you?' asked Sal.
Lola nodded, still out of breath.
'Maybe we should take a look,' Lennie said, slowly.
Lola held his arm.
'I – told you – not to come this – way,' she gasped.

Tim said the man might have been Dracula out for a walk, but no one thought it was funny. Lennie had to admit he'd lost his way. They were all happy to get back to the bright lights.
'What did he look like?' Sal asked as they walked along the front. 'Did you see his face?'
'He was big, bald and ugly. And he was after me.'
'Don't get carried away,' Lennie said, with a grin. 'You just imagined it.'
'I tell you he was coming for me,' Lola shouted.
'Why?' Elvis asked.
'I don't know why –' Lola began. Then she added, in a low voice: 'Maybe he thought I'd seen something I shouldn't have. Like the candlestick he was holding.'

Their caravans were not far from the prom. In half-an-hour they were back on the site.

'You look like you've seen a ghost,' Lola's mother said when she got back. 'What happened?'

Lola told her.

'Keep away from back streets. I've told you before,' her mother snapped. 'If I were you I'd have an early night.'

* * * * *

It was late next morning when Tim called in a paper shop for a comic and a bar of chocolate. He was just leaving when he saw the board by the wall:

£50,000 BLACKPOOL ANTIQUES RAID

He had walked some way when he had a sudden thought. He turned back to the shop.

Inside, the papers were stacked on a shelf. He picked one up and read the headline. Then, still reading, he paid his money and left the shop.

'I think it's the beach again,' Sal was saying as Tim came up. 'What do *you* say, Lola?'

'As long as there are no baldies,' Lola answered. 'I don't want any more shocks for a while.'

Tim came up and thrust the paper into Lola's hand. 'Well here's one for you. Take a look at that.'

Lola began to read the front-page headline Tim had shown her:

ANTIQUES STOLEN

Over £50,000 worth of priceless antiques were stolen last night from a warehouse in Fenwick Street. This is the third time in less than a year that the building has been broken into.

Police believe the robbery is the work of a gang who are operating in the North West.

Anyone with information please call or ring any police station. All help will be treated in confidence.

Lola didn't speak for a moment. Then she said: 'That was it. Fenwick Street. I saw the name on a wall . . .'
'And you've seen one of them,' Sally interrupted. 'The man with the bald head . . . are you going to the police?'
'I suppose I should,' Lola said. 'I had a good look at him.'
'They can do an identikit,' Tim shouted, getting excited. *'Holiday makers give police vital information. Gang arrested.* I can see the headline now.'
But Sal wasn't excited. She'd run away from home earlier that year and the police had been called in. They told her they didn't want to see her again. Since then Sal wanted nothing to do with the police.
'Do we need to get involved?' she asked.
Lennie came up with Elvis.
'What do you think, Lennie? Shall I ring the police?' It was the

first time Lola had asked Lennie's advice. As soon as he knew what it was all about he knew what she should do.
'You tell them, Lola. Tell them what you saw.' Then, he added, with a grin: 'Who knows? You could get your name in the papers.'

* * * * *

As Lola was giving a description of the man she had seen last night, two figures were making their way round the back of the sideshows at the fair. There weren't many people about, and no one took any notice of them. One was tall and well-built, the other short and stocky. They were carrying a box. A big box, more like a packing case. It was heavy. It took both of them to carry it.
They wore workmen's clothes, and looked as if they worked on the fair. The one in front had a bald head. It didn't seem right on such a big man . . .

* * * * *

'So, just to make sure we've got it right . . .' said the policeman. 'You were going back to your caravans when one of you – Lennie – decided to take you by the short way. Right?'
Lennie grinned and nodded.
'While you were in Fenwick Street, *you*' – he pointed to Elvis – 'saw a light on in the warehouse and told your friends about it. OK?'
'No one took much notice,' said Elvis. 'I thought they were

working late but they couldn't have been. Not *that* late anyway?

'All right,' cut in the policeman, 'Then we come to *you*, Lola. Witness number one. You say you saw the man when you got up after fixing your shoe.'

Lola nodded.

'And you also heard a noise.'

'Yes.'

'What sort of noise? Was it a bang, a thud? What?'

'A sort of scraping sound.'

'Coming from inside the warehouse?'

'Yes. As if something heavy was being moved.'

'But nothing suspicious apart from that.'

'No.'

'The light was still on?'

'Yes.'

'And that would be – around what time, would you say?'

Lennie answered: 'It was just before 10.45. I was checking my watch when Lola ran up.'

The policeman noted it all down.

'Now, the important bit. Tell me about the man.'

A picture of the face she had seen the night before came into Lola's mind.

'He was big,,' she said, 'and well built.'

'How big? As big as me? Bigger?'

'Bigger than you,' said Lola.

The man wrote it down.

'What about his face?'

Lola described the man. She told him about the man's clothing – a light-coloured T-shirt and jeans.

'Any other things you can think of?' asked the policeman, after a moment's silence. 'Earrings, chain – anything else you can remember?'

Lola shook her head. No, that was all. 'Oh, except for one thing.'

'What's that?' asked the man.

'His nose. It was sort of pushed over to one side – as if he'd been in a fight.'

The policeman looked at his notes and read them to Lola to check they were right. The kids moved towards the door.

'Thanks for your help,' he called. 'Lola. I'd like you to stay a while longer. The rest of you can go.

Lola shrugged. She'd had enough of the police station, but she had no say in the matter.

'How long will I be?'

The policeman looked at the desk clock.

'Not long.'

Lola asked the others to wait for her outside, and they went out. Lola was alone with the policeman and a policewoman who'd just come in. She brought cups of tea and the policeman took a seat by Lola's side.

'You've been very helpful,' he told her. 'And I don't want you to feel upset or scared about what I'm going to say.'

The policewoman handed him a book, opened half way

through. There were eight faces on each of the two pages. Each face was shown from the side and from the front. 'Do you recognise the man you saw? Is he one of these people?' the policewoman asked.

'That's him!' Lola pointed to the face on the top right. Lola brought her eye close to the picture. She nodded, surprised. 'Yes. That's him – but how – ?'

'There are quite a few bald crooks, but not many with a bent hooter,' said the policeman. 'Fred Perks.' He snapped the book shut. 'It's a long time since we had the pleasure of his company.' He looked hard again at Lola. 'To get back to what I was saying. This Perks is a crook and an ugly one at that. Now we'll probably pick him up within 24 hours, but in the meantime it may be best if you lie low.'

'What do you mean?' asked Lola. 'I'm not the crook.'

'No, you're not,' answered the policeman. 'But Fred can get a little bit nasty at times, and he has seen you from close up. He doesn't *know* you've been to the police. But if he sees you about and thinks you *might* have come here, he could get nasty. Understand?'

'You mean he's dangerous?'

'I mean keep with the crowds, stay with your mates, don't go out alone. The chances of you running into him are slim, but don't be silly. Fred's a local lad, not into the big time. He'll stick around. Here, in Blackpool. Just don't go looking for trouble. Right?'

They were all under the pier. Lola told them what the policeman had said.

'I shouldn't worry,' Lennie told her. 'We're going home tomorrow anyway. He won't recognise you again –'

'Tell you what,' interrupted Tim. 'We've been here all week and never been up the Tower. How about we give it a go before we leave?'

'When?' asked Elvis.

'What's wrong with now?' answered Tim, with a grin. 'That OK, Lennie?'

Lennie grinned back. 'It's fine by me,' he said. 'Let's go.' It was a big adventure, just what Lola needed to take her mind off last night. Within five minutes they were climbing into the lift and moving up. Somewhere below, in the mass of people walking along the front, was a tall, well-built man. A man with a broken nose and a bald head.

* * * * *

It was 10 o'clock at night. The sea was as calm as a pond and through the glare of lights the stars shone. Lennie stopped by the pier and the rest grouped around him. 'I vote we have a count-up,' he said. 'Let's see how much money we've got left.'

'What for?' asked Elvis.

'To see what we can afford,' Lennie answered, his eyes twinkling. 'It's the last night. We can pool what we've got left, split it between us.'

'Then what?' asked Sal, who didn't like the idea.
'Then decide what to do when we find out we're rich.' Lennie answered.

But they were poor. Between them they had just £10. 'That's two pounds each,' Lennie said. 'So it looks like the fair – and forget food. We can't afford any.'
'Hey – hang on, this is *your* idea,' Lola broke in, her eyes flashing. 'I don't remember being asked for my opinion. Maybe I don't want to go to the fair.'
'And I'm not parting with *my* money,' Sal shouted. 'I've got over £4 and I'm buying my mum something before we go back. *I'm* not sharing.'
Lennie grinned. 'OK, I was just stirring,' he said. He took his wallet out of his pocket and pulled out five £5 notes. 'I've been saving,' he told them. 'Tonight is on me – as long as we make it the fair. Agreed?'
They couldn't believe their luck. Even Lola had to smile. 'Well, when you say it like that we have to say yes, don't we?'
'Just remember what you were told this morning,' Lennie reminded her, not grinning now. 'We stay together as much as we can. Right?'

The crowds moved through the pools of light. There was a mixture of sounds. Screams from people on the high rides, the rumble of dodgems, the tinkle of coins. Over everything came the beat of music. All around lights flashed. The big wheel turned slowly, its red, yellow and blue bulbs hanging against the stars. There was the pop of rifles, the hum of electric motors. Excitement.

'OK,' said Lennie, 'Hold out your hands.'

He gave everyone a fiver.

'Now don't say I never give you anything.'

Tim was going to ask if Lennie had helped with the warehouse job, but decided it was too noisy for jokes.

Lola couldn't believe it. £5 in her hand. 'Right, Lennie. I take back all I've said about you behind your back. I fancy the chair-a-plane to start with. What about you, Sal?'

Sal couldn't get over Lennie's hand-out. She thought he'd flipped. Lola was already pulling her along.

'Stick together!' Lennie shouted after them. But he was wasting his breath. Within a minute the girls were spinning through the air.

But it wasn't the ride that made Lola's heart miss a beat.

It was someone she'd glimpsed against the rifle range. She saw him as the plane took her towards the stars. Someone she'd seen before. A big man with a bald head!

* * * *

'I must try that ride,' Lennie said, as Lola came up. 'Seems like you had a good time back there.'

'It's not the ride, Lennie,' Lola told him.

Lennie's grin faded. There was something in Lola's voice. Something like fear.
Sal said: 'She saw the man.'
Tim looked up. 'You mean old Baldy? The creature from the black pit?'
'Got it in one,' Lola replied, sharply. She pointed towards the

rifle range. 'Just there, talking to someone.'

They looked across. There was a group of four people firing. Two girls, two men. None was very tall, and they all had hair.

'Come on, Lola,' Lennie found his smile at last. 'You've had a funny day, what with the police and all that. You're starting to see things.'

'Yeah,' Elvis agreed. 'People that aren't there.'

Lola's eyes sparkled angrily.

'I tell you I saw him. Over by the guns.' She knew what they were thinking – she'd flipped. 'I tell you he was *there*,' she almost shouted.

Lennie tried to take the heat out of it.

'Lola, it's night-time, you were spinning around 40 feet in the air, lights flashing on and off, music blasting your ears – you *imagined* it. OK? The chances of any of us bumping into Fred Perks are nil. The police have probably got him under lock and key right now –'

'– Chained to the cell wall –' added Tim.

'– with a cannon ball tied to his foot –' agreed Elvis.

Lola's smile came back. Perhaps she was wrong after all.

* * * * *

'OK,' Lennie said. 'What next?'

A vote was taken. It had to be the Switchback. A real nail-biter. Up in the clouds at 60 mph.

'That suit you, Lola?' he asked.
She nodded, grinning.

One car was already climbing the rails. They got into the one behind and waited for it to start. Slowly, their car moved forward. They could hear the wheels clanking on the steel. Up the slope, slowly to the top, then the car swept down.
Sal's fingers were white as she gripped the seat in front. Lola held tight, screaming.
Only Lennie stayed calm. He didn't want to blot out the excitement he'd paid for. He kept his hands free and his eyes open. He was the only one to notice the other car, way below them, coming into the bend. It shot under them, and he followed it briefly with his eyes.

He had only seen Fred Perks in dim light at the end of a dark street, but he wondered if Lola really had been mistaken. He waited for the car to come close again. It happened just before the end of the ride. The first car was crashing down the final slope as their car moved again, slowly, upwards. Lennie grabbed Lola's arm as the first car tore past. He jabbed his finger at it. Lola seemed to understand right away. She yelled 'Yes' as their car plunged down.

Lennie tried to keep an eye on Fred Perks. It wasn't easy. Their car was still on the Switchback. Fred's car stopped at the end.

Lennie saw Fred get out.

Lennie saw Fred walk through the exit.

Lennie saw Fred walk up to another man and clap him on the back.

Then . . . Lennie lost them. Fred and his mate just melted into the crowds.

* * * * *

Their ride on the Switchback finished. They crowded together on the way out.

'That was great,' Sal shouted.
'Didn't look like you enjoyed it,' said Tim.
'But I did!' Sal moved over to hit Tim. She thought he was a real pain, sometimes. Him and his smart mouth.

'STOP IT,' said Lennie, very firmly. 'I have some thinking to do. But first I've got to say sorry to Lola.
The others looked at him. Lennie, saying sorry to Lola!
'Yes,' said Lennie. He turned to Lola. 'You were right. Fred Perks is here. I should have believed you. Sorry.'

Lola just looked at Lennie for a long time. Then, 'That's OK,' she said.

'How do you know he's here?' asked Sal.

'Because – I – saw – him. OK?' Lennie said, very slowly. 'And because Lola saw him, too. On the Switchback. He's here all right.'
'So, what do we do about him?' asked Elvis. 'He's dangerous. The police said so.'

Lennie looked at Elvis. 'Here's what we do. We stick together. We stay close. If we see him, we tail him.'

'Tail him?' shrieked Elvis. 'We're supposed to tell the police!'

'OK,' said Lennie. *'We'll* tail him. *You,*' and he pointed at Elvis, 'go tell the police. Go and find the police. Tell them Fred Perks is here. Tell them to get here fast!'

'But where do I *find* the police . . .?' Elvis didn't sound sure.

'Just use your brains. That stuff between your ears,' Lennie snapped. 'And be quick!'

Elvis darted into the crowd.

Lola looked worried. 'Should we really get mixed up in all this?' she said. 'You know what the police said to me – about him being bad news . . .'

Lennie grinned. 'Don't you want to be famous? Have your name in the papers?'

'Yes,' said Lola, 'but not as a dead body. *Murder victim found in fairground* is not how I want to be in the papers. Fred Perks is *dangerous*, Lennie.'

Lennie looked serious. 'Look, Lola,' he said, 'Fred Perks scared you. I don't like people who scare my friends. And I don't like baddies, either. We'll find him and tail him. If we stay together, we'll be OK. What do you think, Tim?'
Tim just smiled. He was nervous. He didn't feel like smiling.
'What do you think, Sal?' asked Lennie.
Sal didn't say anything. She was staring at the bumper cars. 'Don't look now,' she whispered, 'but I think I can see him!'

Lennie turned round slowly. There, in a red car in the middle of a smash, was Fred Perks. His mate was in the car with him. They were laughing.

Lennie grinned. He could feel his skin tingle with excitement. Like a gang of hunters, they trailed their prey through the lights and shadows. Fred Perks was always in front of them. His mate was like his shadow. Fred laughed like a crazy person as he tried each ride. He went into the hall of mirrors. They heard him talking to himself. They imagined him. Big head – short body. Short head – long body. Long head – long body. Fat head – fat body . . .

* * * * *

Elvis was unlucky. He couldn't find a single policeman. He couldn't find a phone. He didn't dare ask any of the fairground people for help. They might be mixed up with Fred Perks.

So Elvis walked all the way to the police station.

'We've found Fred Perks,' he shouted as he pushed open the door. The policewoman on duty didn't know what he was talking about. The minutes ticked by as he tried to explain.

* * * * *

'There he goes!'
It was Sal who saw him. Fred Perks was at the gate into the Ghost Train. Fred and his mate were through the gate. They were waiting for the next car.
'We must follow him,' said Lennie. 'Let's go.'
'You're going to follow him *inside*?' Lola gasped.
'Not me. All of us!' said Lennie. 'Come on, or we'll lose him.'
Lennie was enjoying himself. He'd forgotten about the danger. He'd forgotten about the policeman's warning to Lola. He'd forgotten Fred Perks was bad news. He'd forgotten everything except the hunt. He *had to catch Fred Perks.*

* * * * *

'You say what?' The policewoman looked over the desk at Elvis. Elvis was trying to make her understand.

'It's about the antiques raid. The one in Fenwick Street. It was in the papers. We were here this morning. The man was Fred Perks. He's at the fair now. You must get down there, or it'll be too late. They're with him now. They're tailing him. Lennie, Lola, all of them...'

'Hold on,' said the policewoman. 'Let's start at the beginning...'
'If we start at the beginning it'll be the end for Lennie and Lola and Sal and Tim. You must help us!' Elvis shouted.

'From the beginning...' said the policewoman.

* * * * *

Fred and his mate were in the queue. Ghost cars banged through the doors with screams and shouts from the people inside. A green light shone on and off across the rails, lighting the crowd below. Weird noises came from the tunnel.

A car stopped. People got out of it, laughing. Fred and his mate climbed in, with another man. As the car went through the doors, Lennie, Lola, Sal, and Tim burst through the line, and before anyone could stop them they jumped into the next car and were through the doors.

Suddenly it was very dark. Spiders' webs brushed their faces. A light flashed on. And off. Then on again, and they saw the pale shape of a monk. He didn't have a face. He had a skull. The car moved on, throwing them this way and that. There was a ghostly laugh, then a blood-curdling scream. The car shot past a witch. Her long nails slashed at Sal's face. The witch vanished as the light went out. The car cut through the darkness.

Suddenly . . . the car stopped. A faint green light began to glimmer just in front. There were three shadows in the light. They were still. One held a knife which gleamed like a bright cut in the darkness.

'Murderers!' Tim gasped, not sure. 'Don't they look real, Lennie?' His voice was little more than a whisper. But the whisper turned to a cry of horror as the man with the knife began to move.

* * * * *

Elvis was still in the police station.
'But you know all about the antiques raid. In Fenwick Street. We told you about it this morning.' Elvis was

shouting. 'Why do you want me to tell you again?'

'I must have the details,' said the policewoman.

Just then the door opened. Elvis turned round. The man who walked in was the same policeman they'd seen that morning. Elvis jumped up and ran towards him. *'You* know!' said Elvis, fiercely. 'You know about the antiques and Fred Perks and Lola and . . .'

'Hold on,' said the policeman. 'Let's start at the beginning . . .'

'Oh no!' gasped Elvis, 'I don't believe this! You remember Fred Perks?'

'Yes,' said the policeman. 'And the Fenwick Street antiques.'

'Well, we came in this morning. Lola saw it all . . .' Elvis told his story again. When he had finished things began to move.

It was Elvis's first (and maybe his last) ride in a police car. They raced to the fair. The sirens wailed. The lights on the roof flashed blue beams across the fairground.

* * * * *

'I suppose you thought you were clever,' snarled Perks. 'But I'm cleverer. I spotted you before you spotted me. And you came right into my trap. Just like rats!' Perks flashed the knife dangerously. The two men with him were grinning in the dim light. At their feet there were two large crates. 'And now you've seen too much. And people what see too much have to be made quiet. Right, lads?'

'I shouldn't try it, Fred.' Lennie sounded braver than he felt. 'She gave the police your description.' He nodded towards Lola. 'They're on their way.'

The big man laughed. 'That bluff won't work with me, kid. And even if you weren't bluffin', there's no way they'd find me here.'

Lennie shrugged his shoulders. 'It's up to you,' he said. 'They're all around. You'll get five years. Who's bothered?'

Perks took a step closer. He was a giant. He towered over them. Tim was shaking with fear. The girls were trembling. Perks grabbed Lennie by the coat and pushed the point of the blade into the boy's chin.

'Seems you're more dangerous than the girl,' he scowled. 'Still it doesn't much matter. We'll leave the stuff here for now. No one'll ever find it. Right. Grab them.'

His two mates came up.

'Let's go,' Perks said. 'Move!'

He jabbed with the point of the blade, making Lennie cry out. His mates grabbed the others. One had Sal and Tim. The other had Lola. They had the strength of bears.

'The back way,' ordered Fred.

Sal was crying by now. The man who held her had a grip like steel.

'Where are you taking us?' Lola screamed, struggling and lashing out with her feet.

'You'll see,' the big man laughed. Then he added: 'It might be the last thing you see . . .'

The police had blocked all the exits.
'They were here,' Elvis said. 'I left them here.'
The police moved out to search the fair.
A fair-ground worker saw the police and had a sudden thought. Pushing through the knots of staring people he grabbed a policeman by the arm and pointed to the Ghost Train shed. 'The train's broken down,' he said. 'It's never happened before. Maybe it's nothing, but –'
They moved towards the Ghost Train.

* * * * *

Fred pushed them through the gloom.
One of the men began to get nervous. 'We'd better fix the train, Fred. Get it working again. They'll smell a rat.'
A slow smile spread over Fred's face. He pulled a fuse from his pocket and pushed it into a box on the wall. With a jerk the empty cars set off. Fred clicked on a torch.
'You worry too much,' he told his mate. 'It's bad for you.'
They could hear the cars crashing through the tunnels. Fred was pulling Lennie at knife-point, the other three followed behind, pushed by the two men. They could hear the thunder of cars on the far side, and the wild screams of the people in them. They pushed past a Frankenstein's monster. It's eyes shone like red lamps, and it bent towards them.
Suddenly, Fred kicked at the wall and a door sprung open. They were out in the open air at the back of the Ghost

Train buildings.

'Which way, Fred?'

As he asked the question, the man eased his grip on Lola's arm. It was just the break she'd been waiting for. She suddenly kicked at the man's leg. He gave a yelp of pain and grabbed his knee. Lola turned and ran. She tripped over a cable and fell against someone. She groaned. Then, looking up, she saw it was a policeman.

* * * * *

Well, there you are. Fred's doing time now, with the others. All the stuff's back safe and sound. As for me – well, I just carry on working as usual.

I don't suppose anything like that will happen again. Still, you never know. Sometimes I think Fred Perks is brighter than he looks. I mean, to think up a plan to get a job in the fair, then hide the stuff in the Ghost Train – quite clever, don't you think?

Lucky I grabbed that policeman by the arm when I did. Yes, it was me – the fairground worker. The one who's been telling you all this. It was just an idea – but it paid off.
She had plenty of spirit, that girl Lola. In fact, I think they all had – in their own way.

I wouldn't be surprised if you didn't hear from them again.